EVEN MORE

NONSENSE

FROM Michael Rosen

EVEN MORE
NonSense

FROM Michael Rosen

Illustrated by
Clare Mackie

Wayland

an imprint of Hodder Children's Books

Dedications

For Eddie – Michael Rosen

IN HAPPY AND LOVING MEMORY OF
MINTY AND DAVID AND ALDRIC. C.M.

First published in Great Britain in 2000 by
Hodder Wayland, an imprint of
Hodder Children's Books

Poems © Michael Rosen
Illustrations © Clare Mackie

Edited by Wendy Knowles
Designed by Ian Butterworth

A Catalogue record for this book is available from the British Library.

ISBN 0 7502 2880 6

Printed and bound in Edições ASA, Portugal

Hodder Children's Books
A division of Hodder Headline Limited
338 Euston Road, London NW1 3BH

CAT

THE INVISIBLE CAT

BEE CONTENT(S)

2 BEE OR NOT 2 BEE

INTRODUCTION......6

SOMETHING THAT SMELLS......7

WALKING HOME......8

P.C.CATS......10

PLONKY WONKY DOODAH......11

MY FRIEND ELSIE......12

THE GREAT BIG HOLE......13

THE CAT WENT OUT......14

THANK YOU FOR THE GRAPES......16

WANNABEES.....17

YOU THINK YOU KNOW......17

THE SMEENGE......18

LITTLE QUEENIE......20

TONY CROSS......21

RIDING DOWN TO BOXLAND.....22

THE INVISIBLE CAT JOKES......24

INKY STINKY......25

MY DRINK......26

WINDSCREEN WIPERS......28

OUR PARTY......29

TREASURE......30

AN END TO ALL THIS NONSENSE......32

I remember bee-friending Elsie!

BEE - BOP.

That'll be the bee all and end all!

A bee-fitting introduction Michael!

INTRODUCTION K?

It's got nothing to do with me Michael!

Ithink that an introduction is something to do with a duck. I think an introduction is what happens when a duck dives into the water. So far, after looking all round the world and in many, many ponds I have not yet found anyone who agrees that an introduction is what happens when a duck goes into water. So I ask myself, am I completely wrong? Maybe an introduction is something else altogether. I think I will go on another trip round the world to find out what it really is. By the way, this is a book of nonsense. I once did a book that was called a *Book of Nonsense*. This one is called *Even More Nonsense*. I wonder if this means that the nonsense in this new book is more even? That's all for now.

What does he mean more EVEN? It all sounds very ODD to me!

Michael Rosen

It sounds un-bee-lievable to me.......

Something That Smells

Something that smells,
we call a scent.
Two things that smell
we call scents.
So something that doesn't smell
we can call a non-scent
and two things that don't smell
we can call non-scents.
If you ask me
this sounds like nonsense.

Do you know why we stink?

It's our instinct.

BEE - GIN HERE

7

Walking Home

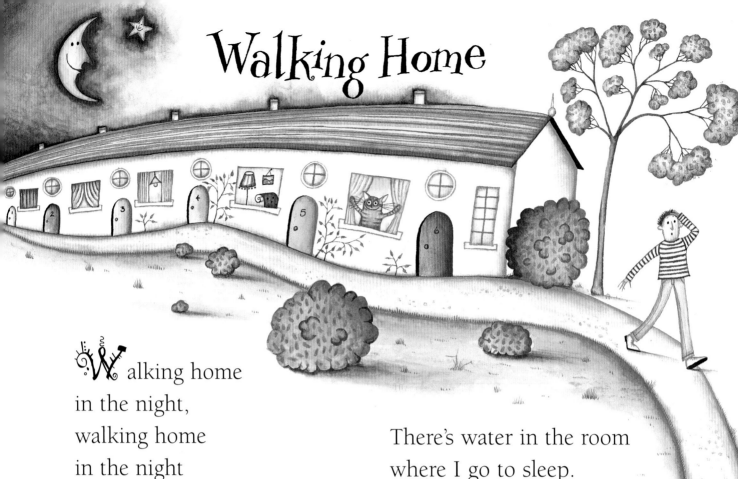

Walking home
in the night,
walking home
in the night
looking into houses
seeing all the lights.

Lights in the windows
lights in the doors
lights up the stairs
lights on all the floors.

But my house is odd.
My house is strange.
The moment I reach home
I can see that it's changed.

There's water in the room
where I go to sleep.
Water water everywhere
water really deep.

There's a man in the kitchen
I see him swimming past.
There's a girl in the lounge.
Oh, she's swimming fast.

There are people upstairs
splashing water at each other.
There's a girl in the window
splashing her little brother.

BEE-CAUSE

And swimming round and round
my bedroom wall
is my Uncle Jack
with his old beach ball.

And isn't that my neighbour's daughter?
Yes, that's my neighbour's daughter.
She's come round for a swim
'cos my house is full of water.

My house is not a house.
I feel such a fool.
I used to live here,
but my house is now a pool.

Plonky Wonky Doodah

Plonky Wonky Doodah
chatting online,
Plonky Wonky Doodah
chatting all the time,
Plonky Wonky Doodah
computer nerd.

Plonky Wonky Doodah
'Don't be so rude!'
Plonky Wonky Doodah
'It's time for your food!'
Plonky Wonky Doodah
hasn't even heard.

P.C. on earth
and goodwill to
all users!

I ♥ P.C's

I'm bored.

Is that a
B-mail for me?

13

My Friend Elsie

My friend Elsie
got very hot.
My friend Elsie
got a big spot.

My friend Elsie
started to drink.
My friend Elsie
started to stink.

My friend Elsie
went all red.
My friend Elsie
went to bed.

My friend Elsie
had to stay in.
My friend Elsie
got very thin.

My friend Elsie
in the midnight hour.
My friend Elsie
turned into a flower.

Hi, Elsie!

My friend Elsie
smells so sweet.
My friend Elsie
has lost her feet.

My friend Elsie
has lost her boots.
My friend Elsie
has grown deep roots.

Has anyone seen Elsie?

12

The Great Big Hole

Look at the road!
Look at the road!
Right in the middle
is a great big hole.

What shall we do?
What shall we do
when we get close
to the great big hole?

I walk round,
I walk round
right round the edge
of the great big hole.

But you fall in,
you fall in.
You disappear
in the great big hole.

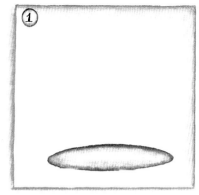

Now there's me!
Now there's me!
Just me on my own

and a great big h○le.

13

TAB-BEE

The Cat Went Out

The cat went out on a chilly night
And looked up at the distant stars.
'Why should I live at 23?
I'd rather live on Mars.

I could go wherever I want.
I could become a stray.
I could stay at 49
or walk The Milky Way.'

The telescope she had
from the man at 33
she pointed at the sky
to see what she could see.

'Oh no! Oh yes!' she gasped,
stunned by what was there,
for high in the heavens above
was the gleaming Planet Chair.

14

She whisked her whiskers
and twitched her face
'I'll be the world's first
Stray Cat in Space.'

And she did just that.
Her rocket took her there.
She steered it down
and landed on the chair.

So go out tonight,
look up at the stars above
and you might see the cat
sitting on the chair she loves.

Zooming round the earth
at a million miles an hour
was a comfy yellow chair
trailing a golden shower.

She stared at it spinning:
'I want to fly up there
I want to get near enough
to sit on that lovely chair.

I'll put some milk in a flask
and a fish in my pocket
I'll find me a helmet
and take off in a rocket.'

MILKY WAY

SATURN

THE PLOUGH

CHAIR..

15

Thank You For The GRAPES

VITAMIN B

Thank you for the grapes.
The grapes are great.
Thank you for the grapes.

No matter how many I pick...
The grapes are great.
No matter how many I pick...

I pull a grape off the bunch.
The grapes are great.
I pull a grape off the bunch.

...the bunch stays just the same,
...the bunch stays just the same,

I put the grape in my mouth.
The grapes are great.
I put the grape in my mouth.

The grapes are great
The grapes are great.

I go back to the bunch.
The grapes are great.
I go back to the bunch.

And the bunch is just the same.
The grapes are great.
The bunch is just the same.

I'm a fat cat who likes fat grapes.

Grape Expectations

WE'RE HAVING A GRAPE TIME!

16

You Think You Know

Wannabees

HONEY BEE

MONEY BEE

RUNNY BEE

SUNNY BEE

FUNNY BEE

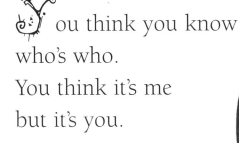

You think you know
who's who.
You think it's me
but it's you.

You think you know
where we are.
You think it's near
but it's far.

You think you know
when it is.
You think it's mine
but it's his.

You think you know
why I don't.
You think I will
but I won't.

You think you know
what's what.
You think I'm here
But I'm not.

What are you talking about?

17

The Smeenge

'The smeenge, the smeenge
what is the smeenge?'
The parents ask the child.
'It's big, it's small.
It's round, it's square.
It's kind of, sort of wild.'

'The smeenge, the smeenge
what is the smeenge?'
The parents want to know.
'It's loud, it's quiet.
It sits, it runs.
It's kind of, sort of slow.'

'The smeenge, the smeenge
what is the smeenge?'
The parents want an answer.
'It jumps, it leaps.
It growls, it purrs.
It's a kind of, sort of dancer.'

& nice tights!

18

'The smeenge, the smeenge
where is the smeenge?'
The parents are in despair.
'It's up, it's down.
It's there, it's here.
It's kind of, sort of everywhere.'

'The smeenge, the smeenge
what is the smeenge?'
The parents don't know what.
'It's a thing, I think.
A think, I thing.
I've kind of sort of forgot.'

Hi!

R.I.P.   R.I.P.   R.I.P.

R.I.B.

Hi heels.

19

ABC

Little Queenie

Little Queenie, Little Queenie, you know you're a meany
sitting in the middle
of a great big hall.
Little Queenie, Little Queenie, you know you're a meany
hating the way
you're much too small.

You think if you pick on someone very big
someone much
bigger than you,
you think if you pick on someone very big
that you will
get very big too.

You yell and you shout, you boss us about
screaming till your face
goes blue.
You yell and you shout, you boss us about
but we know what
you're trying to do.

Little Queenie, Little Queenie, you know you're a meany
but nothing you do
ever works.
Little Queenie, Little Queenie, you know you're a meany
but nothing you do
ever hurts.

Tony Cross

Tony Cross
Tony Cross
please don't make
Tony cross.

Tony Mann
Tony Mann
it's real cool
Tony, man.

Tony Currie
Tony Currie
did you give
Tony curry?

Tony Reed
Tony Reed
ask the teacher,
'Can Tony read?'

Tony George
Tony George
'George, meet Tony!
Tony, George.'

Tony Watt
Tony Watt
you'll give
Tony what?

Tony Hurd
Tony Hurd
do you know
what Tony heard?

Tony Wilde
Tony Wilde
the naughty cat
made Tony wild.

Riding Down To Boxland

Riding down to boxland
where people live in boxes,
riding down to boxland
the people live in boxes,
no chickens there,
been eaten by the foxes.

Riding down to boxland
saw a box looking good,
riding down to boxland
found a box looking good,
wanted to knock on the box
wondered if I should.

Riding down to boxland
I knocked on the lid,
riding down to boxland
knock, knock on the lid,
though I knocked loud
you'd never know I did.

Riding down to boxland
no answer from inside,
riding down to boxland
not a sound from inside,
I picked up the box
to take it for a ride.

Riding back from boxland
the box coming with me,
riding back from boxland
the box coming with me,
laid it out at home,
for everyone to see.

When I got back from boxland
everyone was there.
I was back from boxland
everyone was there,
no one looked inside
there's no one who dared.

FOR YOU

IF I COULD GET CHICKEN POX WHAT KIND OF POX WOULD A FOX ON A BOX GET?

FRAGILE – DO NOT LEAN BIKES HERE

WHY NOT TRY THIS WAY UP TOO

OR THIS WAY UP

COULD BE THIS WAY TOO

THIS WAY UP

PLEASE KNOCK BEFORE LOOKING

23

The Invisible Cat Jokes

Inky Stinky

Inky Stinky Skull Face
doesn't like his Dad.
Inky Stinky Skull Face
thinks his Dad is bad.

Hobbly Bobbly Pimple Chops
looks like Stinky's Dad,
so Inky Stinky Skull Face
thinks Hobbly Bobbly's bad.

MY DAD'S BAD

My Drink

YuK!

My drink started to stink
my dumpling was crumpling.

Dinner disaster
dinner disaster
my head was spinning
faster and faster.

My bread was turning red,
my peas began to sneeze.

Faster and faster
faster and faster
we were heading
for dinner disaster.

My eggs were growing legs
my beans were wearing jeans
my pie winked its eye
my rice was chasing mice.

At half past five
my dinner was alive.
At half past eight
so was my plate.
At the end of the day
my dinner ran away.

No more dinner
no more dinner,
this happens every day
and I'm getting thinner.

Thinner and thinner
thinner and thinner
my dinner runs away
almost every day.

27

Windscreen Wipers

My windscreen wipers don't want to wipe.
They're old and tired and need a rest.
They've swished and swashed for years and years
they think they've done their best.

So I took them off and brought them home
and gave them each a chair.
They sit and watch old movies,
or simply sit and stare.

They do: 'The Snake Who Cleaned Windows':
the 'Windscreen Vipers' joke.
They talk of scrapes and dangers
like the time the windscreen broke.

They read the papers, have a stretch
and after they have fed
they have a wash, clean their teeth
and settle down in bed.

My windscreen still gets dirty and wet,
it looks smarter than it's been.
Two new wipers, strong and fast
wipe the windscreen clean.

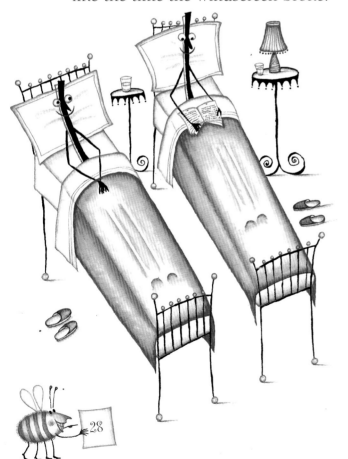

Who am I? Why am I here?
What's going on?

To question or not to question
that is the BEE

28

Our Party

Come to our party!
It's gonna be a crazy thing.
You won't have to dance,
you won't have to sing.

Come to our party!
Please don't make a mess.
Come how you like
no need for fancy dress.

Come to our party!
Don't bring beers.
Please bring your sobs,
please bring your tears.

Come to our party!
Come for a shout.
Come for an hour,
cry your eyes out.

Come to our party!
You'll cry and cry.
We've got plenty of water
so you won't get dry.

Come to our party!
Come for the night
'cos it's time to cry
with all your might.

What's up with them?

Search me..

So glad I wasn't invited

I suspect the weather may change soon in BAR-BEE-DOS...

(SUN BEE-THING IN) → BAR-BEE-DOS

29

Treasure

CAT PILLAR

CATERPILLAR

I knew a woman who looked for treasure.
She said she did it just for pleasure.
To me that sounded a little bit funny.
I'm sure she was after a load of money.

One day she was digging an old football pitch –
an odd place to dig if you want to get rich.
Better to dig in castles and forts
but a few feet down she found some shorts.

She realised as the shorts were uncovered
something special had been discovered.
No question about it – this was a stunning find
they were giant shorts for a giant behind.

Straightaway the shorts were shown on TV
all over the world crowds gathered to see
these incredible shorts from underground,
the biggest shorts that have ever been found.

The experts appeared to talk us through:
'Someone wore these shorts, we can't say who.
They may have been rich, maybe poor.
A footballer perhaps. Or a dinosaur.'

Soon there were pictures of the shorts being worn
Explanations of why they were torn.
Giant footballers scoring brilliant goals
Cartoons with arrows pointing to the holes.

Everyone thinks they've got the answer, or nearly,
but no one knows anything about them really.
People keep pretending they are seriously wise
about underground shorts of an incredible size.

And I know this sounds a little bit soppy
but a museum in Florida made a copy.
To show that the shorts were really wide
they say, a whole school climbed inside.

The woman I'm afraid never got rich,
the government closed the football pitch.
There's a book called: 'Shorts in Ancient History',
but to tell the truth it's all a mystery.

Do mind that hole!

SHORTS IN ANCIENT HISTORY

①

②

BIGGEST SHORTS EVER FOUND – EVER!

31

A bee-fitting ending
bee-lieve ....so bee it!

An END to all this NON(S)ENSE!

32

That Michael Rosen doesn't know how to bee-hive himself...!...

This bee is tired.
This bee is flagging.